From Wi[...]
to Pro[...]
5778-2[...]

Hebrew — cooses over.

New prophetic Mantle
for prophetic Revelat[...]
is important
There must be wildernes
Face — off
Mat. 3 — 4

Bible Prayers

The Ultimate Life Changing Devotional

Portland — prophetic
portal
Prov. 29:18
Activate the gift
of prophecy
Bring it to them delivers
legalism is gone
Faith is link with
the x spleen
Acts 17
Ability to see feather
than we received

We greeted him & pull
Him into reality.
We prophecy according to
our faith.
Faith starts coming
in new way.
Laws of redemption &
restoration
This year I am moving
into perfect timing
Enemy wants to change
times & laws
We are reestablishing
God's time.
Again is season of
watery
5770 - 5779
2009 - 2019
breaking out of capti-
vity season of Angels
season of sending
season of Jo
season of Breaker
all captivity
Angels are close
Feb. 6

Spiritual resources are giving to me.
Remove reproach
10 yrs. of Apostolic Restoration
Gate is opening to go through

Bible Prayers

Rev. 12

The Ultimate Life Changing Devotional

Move forward in Faith
passing through the Gate

By

Dr. Aaron S. Winter

This year. 3 yr war zone

Hearts of Fire International Publishing

A ministry of Hearts of Fire International Ministries

Gate
Angels
War/Conflict

Ps. 68:11-12
112:5-8
Time to Prosper

New level of Generals
will release power

57.78
is
year of Energy

www.heartsoffireintl.com

1 Cor. 16:9
Mat. 3, 9, 11
John 2, 2 Peter 5:8
Acts 12   Rev. 12:9-12

Copyright

The Bible Prayers in this devotional come from Scriptures verses that are paraphrased and altered into personal prayers that are derived from the following translations and used by permission:

Dedication

This book is dedicated first and foremost to God the Father who is the Ancient of Days and sits on the throne of the heavens; to Jesus Christ of Nazareth for ransoming me through the merciful work on the cross, so that I could become a son that stands, serves, and burn as a priest in His Kingdom. Thank You Holy Spirit of God who is the source of all wisdom and revelation.

A close second, is to my beautiful and amazing wife, Shannon, my best friend, whose support throughout the writing of this book was immeasurable. Her purity of heart and faith are always a source of inspiration and strength.

About the Author

Dr. Aaron S. Winter is the President of Hearts of Fire International Ministries & the television host of Hearts of Fire TV. Operating with a powerful anointing with a prophetic edge, his message of walking in God's power and understanding our true identity in Christ has changed lives all over the world through conferences, seminars, revival meetings, and evangelistic crusades that have seen audiences exceed 100,000 people in attendance.

Aaron has authored numerous books, including: Becoming a Heart of Fire, Bible Prayers, God's Kind of Faith and coming soon Heavenly Realities.

Aaron received his Doctorate in Divinity from Destiny Christian University in 2014 and graduated from Portland Bible College in 2003, earning his Bachelor degree in Theology.

Table of Contents

Instructions

This book is written as a devotional that is intended to be read out loud. Faith comes by hearing, and hearing the Word of God; therefore it is crucial to speak these prayers and decrees out loud to receive the full benefit. Again, want to make it clear, the point of this devotional is for you to read this OUT LOUD!!!

Start by choosing a topic from the Table of Contents and begin reading the bible prayers out loud, remembering that life and death are in the power of the tongue, therefore as you confess the Word of God over yourself, you speak life over your entire being.

Note: The Names of God are not Bible prayers but attributes that are ascribed to God throughout Scripture. As you declare to Him who He is, you will gain a greater understanding of who He is and what He does on your behalf.

In the beginning was the Word, and the Word was with God, and the Word was God. **John 1:1**

Faith comes by hearing, and hearing by the Word of God. **Romans 10:17**

I shall not live by bread alone but by every Word that proceeds from the mouth of God. **Matthew 4:4**

Let it be to me according to Your Word. **Luke 1:38**

Jesus, open my understanding, that I might comprehend Your Word. **Luke 24:45**

I believe in the Scriptures and the words You have spoken. **John 2:2**

Your testimonies I take as an inheritance forever, for they are the rejoicing of my heart. **Psalm 119:111**

Oh, how I love Your Word! **Psalm 119:97**

My heart stands in awe, it trembles at Your Word. **Psalm 119:161**

How sweet are Your Words to my taste, sweeter than honey to my mouth! **Psalm 119:103**

When Your words come, I will eat them: they are my joy and my heart's delight, for I bear Your name. **Jeremiah 15:16**

My delight is in the Word of the Lord, and in Your Word I will meditate both day and night. I will be like a tree planted by rivers and waters, I will bring forth my fruit in its season, my leaf will not wither; and whatever I do will prosper. **Psalm 1:2-3**

I will shine like the stars in the universe as I hold out the Word of Life. **Philippians 2:15:16**

For the Word of God is alive and powerful, and sharper than any two-edged sword, dividing between the soul and spirit, joints and marrow, and is a discerner of the thoughts and intents of my heart. **Hebrews 4:12**

The Holy Scriptures are able to make me wise for salvation through faith, which is in Christ Jesus. All Scripture is given by inspiration of God, and is profitable for doctrine, for reproof, for correction, for instruction in righteousness, that I a man of God may be complete, thoroughly equipped for every good work. **2 Timothy 3:15-17**

Your word is a lamp to my feet, and a light to my path. **Psalm 119:105**

I will keep my way pure by living according to Your Word. I put Your Word in my heart, so I will not sin against You. **Psalm 119:9-11**

Direct my steps by Your Word, and let no iniquity have dominion over me. **Psalm 119:133**

The Word of Christ will dwell in me richly in all wisdom. **Colossians 3:16**

My heart is set on keeping your decrees to the very end. **Psalm 119:12**

Chapter Two

The Spirit of God

In the last days, God says, I will pour out my Spirit on all people. Your sons and daughters will prophesy, your young men will dream dreams. Even on my servants, both men and women, I will pour out my Spirit. **Joel 2:20, Acts 2:17**

The Holy Spirit will come upon me, and the power of the Most High will overshadow me. **Luke 1:35**

I will not leave, but wait for the gift my Father promised, which I have heard Jesus speak about. For John baptized with water, but in a short while I will be baptized by the Holy Spirit. **Acts 1:4-6**

He will baptize me with the Holy Spirit and fire. **Luke 3:16**

As I ask, it will be given to me, seeking I will find; knocking on the door, it will be opened to me. For everyone who asks receives; he who seeks finds; and to him who knocks the door will be opened. **Luke 11:9-10**

I already know how to give good gifts to my children, how much more my Father in heaven will give the Holy Spirit when I ask Him! **Luke 11:13**

I will receive power when the Holy Spirit comes on me, and I will be Christ's witness in my city, region and nation, and to the ends of the Earth. **Acts 1:8**

A suddenly will occur, a sound like the blowing of a violent wind will come from heaven and fill the entire place where I have come to worship. Then I will be filled with the Holy Spirit and will began to speak in other tongues as the Spirit enables me. **Acts 2:3-4**

After we pray, the place where we meet will be shaken. And we will be filled with the Holy Spirit and speak the Word of God with boldness. **Acts 4:31**

Do not be drunk with wine, but be filled with the Holy Spirit. **Ephesians 5:18**

We are witnesses of these things, and so is the Holy Spirit, whom God has given to those who obey Him. **Acts 5:32**

I am entering the kingdom of God because I am born of water and the Spirit. Flesh gives birth to flesh, but the Spirit gives birth to spirit. **John 3:5-6**

Yet a time is coming and has now come when the true worshipers will worship the Father in spirit and in truth... God is spirit and his worshipers must worship in spirit and truth. **John 4:23-24**

Jesus said: "Whoever drinks the water I give him will never thirst. Indeed, the water I give him will become in him a spring of water welling up to eternal life."**John 4 13-14**

Jesus said: "If anyone is thirsty, let him come to me and drink. Whoever believes in me, as the Scripture has said, streams of living water will flow from within him."**John7:37-38**

Jesus will ask the Father, and He will give me another Counselor to be with me forever- the Spirit of truth. I will know Him, for He lives with me and will be in me. **John 14:15-17**

The Counselor, the Holy Spirit, whom the Father will send in Christ's name, will teach me all things and will remind me of everything Jesus has said. **John 14:26**

The Spirit of truth will guide me into all truth. He will not speak on His own, He will speak only what He hears, and He will tell me what is yet to come. **John 16:13**

Jesus breathed on me and said, "Receive the Holy Spirit. **John 20:22**

God revealed it to me by His Spirit. The Spirit searches all things, even the deep things of God. **1 Corinthians 2:10**

The Spirit of life has set me free from the law of sin and death. **Romans 8:2**

I will live according to the Spirit and have my mind set on what the Spirit desires. The mind of sinful man is death, but the mind controlled by the Spirit is life and peace. **Romans 8:5**

And if the Spirit of Him who raised Jesus from the dead is living in me, then He who raised Christ from the dead will also give life to my mortal body through His Spirit, who lives in me. **Romans 8:11**

The fruit of the Holy Spirit is love, joy, peace, patience, kindness, goodness, faithfulness, gentleness and self-control. **Galatians 6:22-23**

Since I live by the Spirit, I will keep in step with the Spirit. **Galatians 6:25**

Chapter Three

Destiny & Sonship

I know the thoughts I have towards you, says the Lord; to give you a future and a hope. **Jeremiah 29:11**

Nothing will separate me from the love of Christ. In all these things I am more than a conqueror through Him who loves me. **Romans 8:35-37**

I am strong in the Lord and the power of His might. **Ephesians 6:10**

I can do all things through Christ who strengthens me. **Philippians 4:13**

He who began a good work in me will complete it until the day of Jesus Christ. **Philippians 1:6**

He is able to do exceedingly abundantly above all that I could ask or think, according to the power than works in me. **Ephesians 3:20**

There is surely a future hope for me, and my hope will not be cut off. **Proverbs 23:18**

Because I have put my faith in Christ, I will do the works of Christ, and even greater works than these! **John 14:12**

Everything is possible because I believe. **Mark 9:23**

For I did not receive a spirit that makes me a slave again to fear, but I have received the Spirit of sonship. The Spirit Himself testifies with our spirit that we are God's children. **Romans 8:15**

Christ redeemed me, therefore I now have full rights as a son, and because I am a son, the Father sent the Spirit of His Son into my heart. So now I am no longer a slave but a son, and therefore I am an heir. **Galatians 4:4-7**

God has blessed me in the heavenly realms with every spiritual blessing in Christ. For He chose me in Him before the creation of the world to be holy and blameless in His sight. In love He predestined me to be adopted as His son through Christ Jesus, for His pleasure and will. In Him I have redemption through the blood, forgiven of all sins. Having believed, I am marked in Him with a seal, the promised Holy Spirit, who is a deposit guaranteeing my inheritance. **Ephesians 1:3-7; 13-14**

I am no longer a foreigner or alien, but a citizen with God's people and a son in God's household. **Ephesians 2:19**

God raised me up with Christ and seated me with Him in the heavenly realms. **Ephesians 2:6**

For through Christ I have access to the Father by the Spirit. **Ephesians 2:18**

But as many as received Him, to them He gave the right to become children of God, and I am one of those, because I believe in His name. **John 1:12**

Chapter Four

Mountain Moving Faith

And without faith it is impossible to please God. **Hebrews 11:6**

Everything that does not come from faith is sin. **Romans 14:23**

Faith comes by hearing, and hearing by the Word of God. **Romans 10:17**

Now faith is the substance of things hoped for, the evidence of things not seen. **Hebrews 11:1**

I walk by faith and not by sight. **2 Corinthians 5:7**

I am given the ability of faith by the Spirit. **1 Corinthians 12:9**

Out of the abundance of the heart the mouth speaks, therefore I speak words of faith. **Matthew 12:34**

Life and death are the power of the tongue, therefore by faith I speak life. **Proverbs 18:21**

By faith in God, all things are possible. **Mark 10:27**

Jesus said: Anyone who has faith in Me will do greater things than these. **John 14:12**

My actions demonstrate faith, and I have faith that is alive and active in deeds. **James 2:18-24**

I am full of faith and in the Holy Spirit. **Acts 6:5**

I am standing firm in the faith. **1 Corinthians 16:13**

According to my faith it will be done. **Matthew 9:29**

By even the smallest of faith, even that of a mustard seed, I can say to this mountain, 'Move from here to there' and it will be moved. **Matthew 17:20**

With God all things are possible. **Matthew 19:26**

Everything is possible for him who believes. **Mark 9:23**

By faith I understand that the worlds were prepared by the Word of God, so that what is seen was not made out of things which are visible. **Hebrews 11:3**

By faith I stand firm. **2 Corinthians 1:24**

Jesus is the author and finisher of my faith. **Hebrews 12:2**

I pray that out of His glorious riches, that He may be strengthened in me with power through the Spirit in my inner being, so that Christ may dwell in my heart through faith. **Ephesians 3:16-17**

Chapter Five

The Kingdom of Heaven

Yours, O Lord is the Kingdom, You are exalted as head over all. **1 Chronicles 29:11**

I will tell of Your Kingdom, and speak of Your Might. **Psalm 145:11**

Christ's Kingdom is not of this world. **John 18:36**

Jesus declared, "I tell you the truth, no one can see the kingdom of God unless he is born again." **John 3:3**

I am part of His Kingdom of Priests. **Exodus 19:6**

As I go, I will preach this message: The Kingdom of heaven is at hand. **Matthew 10:7**

I will demonstrate the kingdom by healing the sick, raising the dead, cleansing those who have leprosy, and driving out demons. Freely I have received, freely I will give. **Matthew 10:8**

The kingdom of heaven has been forcefully advancing, and forceful men lay hold of it. **Matthew 11:12**

The secret of the kingdom of God has been given to me. **Mark 4:11**

Jesus has given me the keys of the kingdom of heaven; whatever I bind on earth will be bound in heaven, and whatever you loose on earth will be loosed in heaven. **Matthew 16:19**

The kingdom of God does not come with my careful observation, nor will people say, 'here it is,' nor 'there it is,' because Jesus said the kingdom of God is within me. **Luke 17:21**

The kingdom of God is not a matter of eating and drinking and natural things, but of righteousness and joy in the Holy Spirit. **Romans 14:17**

I will not be afraid, for the Father has been pleased to give me the Kingdom. **Luke 12:32**

The kingdom of heaven is like treasure hidden in a field. When a man found it, he hid it again, and then in his joy went and sold all he had and bought that field. Again, the Kingdom of heaven is like a merchant looking for fine pearls. When he found one of great value, he went away and sold everything he had and bought it. Therefore I will look for treasure in God's kingdom and invest everything I am and have. **Matthew 13:44-45**

The kingdom of heaven is like a mustard seed, which a man took and planted in his field. Though it is the smallest of all seeds, yet as it grows, it becomes the largest tree, so all the birds can come and perch in its branches. **Matthew 13:31**

Father in heaven, You are holy and worthy. Establish Yourself on the throne in my heart, that Your kingdom manifests in every aspect of my life, Your will be done by my actions, on earth all around me, just as it is in heaven. **Matthew 6:9-10**

Chapter Six

Power & Authority

God's power is like the working of His mighty strength which raised Him from the dead and seated him at his right hand in the heavenly realms, far above all rule and authority, power and dominion, and every title that can be given, not only in this age but in the one to come. And God has placed ALL things under His feet and appointed Him to be the head over everything. **Ephesians 1:19-21**

And God has (positionally) raised me up with Christ and seated me with Him in the heavenly realms in Christ Jesus. **Ephesians 2:6**

I pray that out of His glorious riches, that He may be strengthened in me with power through the Spirit in my inner being, so that Christ may dwell in my heart through faith. **Ephesians 3:16-17**

Jesus has given me authority to drive out evil spirits and to heal every disease and sickness. **Matthew 10:1**

I receive power when the Holy Spirit who comes upon me and is in me. **Acts 4:8**

I will be filled with the Holy Spirit and speak the Word of God with boldness. **Acts 4:31**

Now, Lord, consider their threats and enable me Your servant to speak Your word with great boldness. Stretch out Your hand to heal and perform miraculous signs and wonders through the name of Your holy servant Jesus. **Acts 4:29-30**

Just like the Apostles, with great power I will continue to testify of the resurrection of the Lord Jesus. **Acts 4:33**

The prayer of a righteous man is powerful and effective and will avail much. Elijah was a man just like me. He prayed earnestly that it would not rain, and it did not rain on the land for three and a half years. And again he prayed, and the heavens gave rain, and the earth produced its crops. **James 5:16**

Chapter Seven

My Victory

Jesus said: The thief does not come except to steal, kill and to destroy. He came that I may have life, and that I may have it more abundantly. **John 10:10**

When the enemy comes, like a flood the Spirit of the Lord will lift up a standard against him. **Isaiah 59:192**

Rise up, O Lord! Let Your enemies be scattered and let those who hate You flee before You. **Numbers 10:35**

I will go up at once and take possession of my land, because in Christ I am well able to overcome it. **Numbers 13:30**

My enemies shall come out against me one way and flee before me seven ways. **Deuteronomy 28:7**

The Lord my God will deliver my enemies over to me, and will inflict defeat upon them until they are destroyed. **Deuteronomy 7:23**

The Lord delivers me from my enemies and lifts me up above those who rise against me. **2 Samuel 22:49**

The Lord my God will give me rest on every side and there will be neither an adversary nor an evil occurrence. **1 Kings 5:4**

I will not need to fight in this battle. I position myself, stand still and will see the salvation of the Lord. I will not fear or be dismayed for the Lord is with me. **2 Chronicles 20:17**

With others is the arm of flesh; but with me is the Lord my God, to help me and to fight my battles. **2 Chronicles 32:8**

I will not be afraid of my enemies because I will remember the Lord who is great and awesome, and stand up and fight for my brothers, my sisters, my children, my spouse, my home and inheritance. **Nehemiah 4:14**

On the day the enemy hopes to overpower me, the opposite will occur because God will turn the table, and I will overpower them. **Esther 9:1**

The Lord prepares a table before me in the presence of my enemies and He anoints my head with oil and my cup runs over. **Psalm 23:5**

I put my trust in You my God; let me not be ashamed and let not my enemies triumph over me. **Psalm 25:2**

When my enemies and my foes come out against me to eat up my flesh, they will stumble and fall. And now my head will be lifted up above my enemies all around me. **Psalm 27:2,6**

By this I know that the Lord is greatly pleased with me, because my enemies do not triumph over me. **Psalm 41:11**

With God I gain the victory, and He tramples down my enemies. **Psalm 60:12**

When my ways please the Lord, He will make even my enemies to be at peace with me. **Proverbs 16:7**

No weapon formed against me shall prevail, every accusation and every mouth that rises up against me, to judge me, I shall condemn. This is the heritage of the servants of the Lord, and my righteousness is from Him. **Isaiah 54:17**

They will fight against me but not overcome me. "For I am with you and will rescue you," declares the Lord. **Jeremiah 1:19**

All of those who devour me, all of my enemies, each and every one, shall go into captivity. Those who have plundered me shall be plundered, and all who prey upon me will be made a prey. Then the Lord will restore me and heal all my wounds. **Jeremiah 30:16-17**

I have authority to trample on serpents and scorpions, and over all the power of the enemy, and nothing shall by any means hurt me or cause me harm. **Luke 10:19**

The God of peace will crush Satan under my feet. **Romans 16:20**

He will reign and put all my enemies under His feet. **1 Corinthians 15:25**

I will overcome my enemies because He who is in me is greater than he that is in the world. **1 John 4:4**

Thanks be to God, who gives me the victory through my Lord Jesus Christ. **1 Corinthians 15:57**

I give thanks to God, who always leads me in triumph in Christ Jesus. **2 Corinthians 2:14**

Through God I will push down my enemies; through His name I will stomp over those who rise up against me. **Psalm 44:5**

I will overcome the devil by the blood of the Lamb, by the word of my testimony and by not loving my life even unto death. **Revelation 12:11**

Chapter Eight

Holiness and Purity

My body is not for sexual sin, but it is for the Lord. I flee sexual sin because every sin I commit is outside of my body, and if I commit sexual sin, I am sinning against my own body. And my body is the temple of the Holy Spirit. I am bought with a price, therefore, I will I will glorify God in my body and in my spirit which are God's. **1 Corinthians 6:18-20**

For this is the will of God, even my sanctification, that I abstain from sexual sin, that I know how to possess my own vessel in sanctification and honor, not in the passion of lust like the gentiles who do not know God; for God did not call me to uncleanness, but to holiness. **1 Thessalonians 4:3-7**

I walk in the Spirit and will not fulfill the lusts of the flesh. And because I am Christ's, I have crucified the flesh with its passions and desires. **Galatians 5:16, 24**

I have clean hands and a pure heart and will not lift up my soul to an idol. **Psalm 24:4**

I set no evil worthless thing before my eyes. **Psalm 101:3**

I have made a covenant with my eyes, why then should I look lustfully upon a woman who is not my wife. Doing so could be a fire that could consume to destruction and root out all my increase. **Job 31:1,12**

By means of an immoral woman I could be reduced to a crust of bread, and an adulteress could prey upon my life. Therefore, I will not lust after her beauty in my heart, nor will I let her seduce me with her eyelids. **Proverbs 6:25-33**

Whoever commits adultery with a woman lacks understanding. The Spirit behind immoral women has wounded and cast down many men, and all who were slain by her were at one time strong. Her house is the way to hell, descending to the chambers of death. **Proverbs 7:26-27**

I will therefore, not give my strength to women, nor my vigor on those who destroys Kings. **Proverbs 31:3**

The mouth of an adulteress is a deep pit; he who is under the Lord's wrath falls into it. **Proverbs 22:13**

I know that whoever looks on a woman with lust in his heart commits adultery with her in his heart, therefore I purpose in my heart that I will not allow my eyes to cause me to stumble, but will be single focused and good, so that my body will be full of light. **Matthew 5:28, 29; 6:22**

Through God's exceedingly great and precious promises, I am a partaker of the divine nature of Christ and have escaped the corruption that is in the world through lust. **2 Peter 1:4**

I will not love the world, nor the things in the world. For all that is in the world, the lust of the flesh, the lust of the eyes and the pride of life are not of the Father, but of the world; and the world is passing away and all of the lust with it. However, because I do the will of God, I will abide forever. **1 John 2:15-17**

I place God's Word in my heart that I might not sin against Him. This is how I am going to keep my way pure, by taking heed to His Word. **Psalm 119,11**

I know that God is not mocked and whatever I sow I reap, therefore I will not sow to the flesh which brings corruption, instead I will sow to the Spirit and reap life everlasting. I will not grow tired in doing good, for in my due season I will reap a plentiful harvest because I will not give up. **Galatians 6:7-9**

I purify my mind, will and emotions by obeying the Truth by the Spirit. I will be self-controlled, girding up the thoughts of my mind as an obedient child, not conforming to my former lusts, as I did in my ignorance, but as he has called me holy, I am holy in all my actions. **1 Peter2:13-15**

I abstain from Sinful lusts which war against my soul- mind, will and emotions. I no longer live the rest of my days in the sin nature for the lusts of the humanity, but for the will of God. **1 Peter 2:11, 4:2**

I will not let sin reign in my mortal body. I will not yield the parts of my body as instruments and weapons of unrighteousness to sin, but I will instead yield the parts of my body as instruments and weapons of righteousness for God. **Romans 6:12-13**

Fornication, uncleanness and idolatry will not even be named in my life, which is proper for Christians. Neither filthiness, nor foolish talking, not even wicked joking around, which are not proper, because I know that no fornicator, unclean person, nor idolater has any inheritance in the Kingdom of God. I let no one deceive me with empty words, for because of these things, the wrath of God comes upon the children of disobedience. Therefore I will not be a partaker with them. **Ephesians 5:3-7**

I walk as a child of light, proving what is acceptable to the Lord. I have no fellowship with the unfruitful works of darkness, but rather expose them. It is shameful for me to even speak of those things which are done by them in secret. **Ephesians 5:8-12**

I put on the Lord Jesus Christ and make no provision for the sin-nature to fulfill its desires. I will act decently in the night just as I would in the day, not partaking in orgies, drunkenness, nor sexual sins, nor fighting nor of jealousies. I cast off the works of darkness and put on the armor of light. **Romans 14:12-14**

I discipline, keep under, subdue my body, bring it into subjection and enslave it; lest after I have witnessed to others, I myself should be cast away, unapproved, disqualified, or rejected. **1 Corinthians 9:27**

Can a man scoop fire into his lap without his clothes being burned? Can a man walk on hot coals without his feet being scorched? So is he who sleeps with another man's wife; no one who touches her will go unpunished. A man who commits adultery lacks judgment, whoever does so destroys himself. **Proverbs 6:27-29, 32**

Lord, I ask that you will incline my heart to Your testimonies, and not to covetousness. That You will turn away my eyes from looking at worthless things, and revive me in Your ways. **Psalm 119:36-37**

My body is the temple of the Holy Spirit who is in me, which I have as a gift from God, and I am not even my own; for I am purchased with a price, therefore I will glorify God in my body and in my spirit, which are God's. **1Corinthians 6:19-20**

Although I live in the flesh, I do not war according to the flesh. For the weapons of my warfare are not carnal, but mighty through God to pull down strongholds, casting down imaginations and every high thing that exalts itself up against the knowledge of God, and I bring into captivity every one of my thoughts, making them obey Christ. **2 Corinthians 10:3-5**

I will not lust after evil things, I will not be an idolater, I will not commit sexual sin, I will not tempt God and I will not whine or complain. I will stand firm in the faith, but stay humble, knowing that it is possible to fall. I know that the temptations that overcome are common to all men; but through that time of temptation, God is faithful, who will not allow me to be tempted beyond what I am able to handle. Therefore He makes a way for me to escape so that I may be able to bear the weight of it. **1 Corinthians 10:6-13**

Whatever is true, noble, just, pure, and lovely and of good report, I am meditating on these things. **Philippians 4:8**

I stand firm in the freedom with which Christ has set me free. I am no longer entangled with a yoke of sinful bondage. **Galatians 5:1**

For I have been called to liberty; however I will not use my liberty as an occasion for the sinfulnature, instead I will serve others in love. **Galatians 5:13**

I walk in the Spirit, and not in the lusts of the flesh. For the sinful nature battles against the Spirit, and the Spirit battles against the sinful nature, and they are contrary to each other; therefore I will be led by the Spirit and partake of the fruit of the Holy Spirit: love, joy, peace, patience, kindness, goodness, faithfulness, gentleness, and self-Control. **Galatians 5:16-17, 22-23**

God says to me: "I will cleanse you from all your impurities and from all your idols. I will give you a new heart and put a new spirit in you; I will remove from you your heart of stone and give you a heart of flesh. And I will put my Spirit in you and move you to follow My decrees and be careful to keep My commands. **Ezekiel 36:25-27**

Chapter Nine

Overcoming Fear

God has not given me a spirit of fear, but of power, love and a sound mind. **2 Timothy 1:7**

I will be delivered from the hand of my enemies and serve the Lord in freedom, without fear. **Luke 1:74**

There is no fear in love. But perfect love drives out all fear, because fear has to do with punishment. **1 John 4:18**

Fear of man will prove to be a snare, but whoever trusts in the Lord is kept safe. **Proverbs 29:25**

I will be strong, and not fear; my God will come, He will come with vengeance, with divine retribution He will come to save me. **Isaiah 35:4**

In God I have put my trust; I will not be afraid. What can man do to me? **Psalms 56:11**

I have favor with God, and will not be afraid. **Luke 1:30**

God says to me: "Do not fear, for I am with you; do not be dismayed, for I am your God. I will strengthen you and help you; I will uphold you with My righteous hand. **Isaiah 41:10**

This is what the Lord says: "Fear not, for I have redeemed you; I have summoned you by name; you are Mine." Therefore when I pass through the waters, He will be with me, they will not sweep over me. When I walk through the fire, I will not be burned, the flames will not set me ablaze; for He is with me. **Isaiah 43:1-2**

I will not be afraid in any man's presence, for the judgment is God's. **Deuteronomy 1:17**

I will do what God says and not fear the reproach of men or be terrified by their insults. **Isaiah 51:7**

I will fear no evil. **Psalm 23:4**

He delivered me from all my fear. **Psalm 34:4**

I will not be afraid; for the Lord will provide for me. **Genesis 50:21**

I will not fear the terror of the night, nor the arrow that flies by day, nor the sickness that stalks in darkness, nor diseases that destroy at midday. A thousand may fall at my side, ten thousand at my right hand, but it will not come near me. **Psalm 91:5-6**

The fear of the Lord is pure. **Psalm 19:9**

The fear of the Lord is the beginning of wisdom. **Proverbs 1:7**

The fear of the Lord is to hate evil. **Proverbs 8:13**

The fear of the Lord is a fountain of life. **Proverbs 14:27**

He will be the sure foundation for my time, a rich store of salvation and wisdom and knowledge; the fear of the Lord is the key to this treasure. **Isaiah 33:6**

I will be like Job and fear the Lord and shun evil. **Job 1:8**

I will fear God and give Him glory. **Revelation 14:7**

You alone are to be feared God. **Psalm 76:7**

Chapter Ten

Forgiveness

I will not judge, or I too will be judged. For in the same way I judge others, I will be judged, and with the measure I use, it will be measured back to me. **Matthew 7:1-2**

Mercy Triumphs over judgment! **James 2:13**

For if I forgive men when they sin against me, my heavenly Father will also forgive me. But if I do not forgive men their sins, my Father will not forgive my sins. **Matthew 6:14**

I will not judge, and I will not be judged. I will not condemn, therefore I will not be condemned. I will forgive, and I too will be forgiven. I will give, and it will be given to me, a good measure, pressed down, shaken together and running over, and will be poured onto my lap. With the measure I use, it will be measured to me. **Luke 6:37-38**

I strive to always keep my conscience clear, without offense, towards God and man. **Acts 24:16**

I will obey Jesus, and love my enemies, do good to those who hate me, bless those who curse and say bad things about me, and pray for those who mistreat me. If they hit me, I will let them hit me again, if they steal, I will only offer them more. I will not repay evil for evil but will be merciful, just as my Father is merciful. **Luke 6:27-29, 36**

I will forgive by brothers and sisters their offenses from my heart. **Matthew 18:36**

I will put away from me all bitterness, resentment, wrath, anger, rage, malice and violence, instead I will be kind to others, tenderhearted, and forgiving others, just as God in Christ forgave me. **Ephesians 4:32**

I will pursue peace with every person, and I will remain humble to prevent the root of bitterness that springs up and causes trouble and even to the point of defiling others. **Hebrews 12:14-15**

I will not seek revenge or bear a grudge against anyone, but love each person as myself. **Leviticus 19:18**

Before I offer a sacrificial gift to God, I will leave my gift in front of the altar and first go and be reconciled to my brother; then come and offer my gift. **Matthew 5:24**

And when I pray, if I hold anything against anyone, I forgive them, so that my Father in heaven may forgive my sins. **Mark 11:25**

Jesus said, "Father, forgive them, for they do not know what they are doing." Therefore I also forgive others who sin against me in ignorance. **Luke 23:34**

And with that Jesus breathes on me and says: "Receive the Holy Spirit. If you forgive others their sins, they are forgiven; if you do not forgive them, they are not forgiven." Therefore in my heart I forgive, that they may be forgiven and I will have the Holy Spirit. **John 20:22-23**

In Him we have redemption through His blood, the forgiveness of sins, in accordance with the riches of God's grace. **Ephesians 1:7**

I bear witness with others and forgive whatever grievances I may have against others, and will strive to make peace with them if I have offended them; to live in a state of forgiveness just as the Lord has forgiven us all. **Colossians 3:13**

Chapter Eleven

Healing and Miracles

God says: For I am the Lord who heals you. **Exodus 15:26**

O Lord my God, I cried out to You, and You healed me. **Psalm 30:2**

You send forth Your word and healed me; You rescue me from the grave. **Psalm 107:20**

He heals the broken hearted and binds up their wounds. **Psalm 147:3**

When I cry out to You God, You reply: "Here I am". **Isaiah 58:8-9**

This is what the Lord, the God of your father David, says: I have heard your prayer and seen your tears; I will heal you, and add to your life fifteen years. **2 Kings 20:5**

I said, "Oh Lord, have mercy on me; heal me, for I have sinned against you." **Psalm 41:4**

He Himself bore our sins in His body on the tree, so that we might die to sins and live for righteousness; by His wounds I have been healed. **2 Peter 2:24**

Praise the Lord, O my soul, and forget not all His benefits- who forgives all my sins and heals all my diseases, who redeems my life from the pit and crowns me with love and compassion, who satisfies my desires with good things so that my youth is renewed like the eagle's wings. **Psalm 103:2-5**

A man was found who had been bedridden for eight years. Then Peter looked at him and said: "Jesus Christ heals you. Get up and pick up your mat." Immediately the man got up. **Acts 9:33-34**

Jesus said to him, "I will go and heal him." The centurion replied, "Lord, I do not deserve to have you come under my roof. But just say the word, and my servant will be healed. For I myself am a man under authority, with soldiers under me. I tell this one, "Go, and he goes; and that one, 'Come,' and he comes. I say to my servant, Do this, and he does it." **Matthew 8:7-9**

Jesus asked the blind men, "Do you believe that I am able to do this?" "Yes, Lord," they replied. Then He touched their eyes and they were healed. **Matthew 9:28-30**

When the sun was setting, the people brought to Jesus all who had various kinds of sickness, and laying His hands on each one, He healed them. **Luke 4:40**

And whenever He went into villages, towns or countryside, they placed the sick in the marketplaces. They begged Him to let them touch even the edge of His cloak, and all who touched Him were healed. **Mark 6:56**

He was wounded for our transgressions, He was bruised for our iniquities; the chastisement for our peace was upon Him, And by His stripes we are healed. **Isaiah 53:5**

I will heal you, says the Lord. **Isaiah 57:19**

Chapter Twelve

God's Love

Love endures long and is patient and kind; love never is envious nor is overcome with jealousy. It never boasts or is vain seeking its own glory. It does not display itself condescendingly in arogance., because love is not conceited & inflated with pride; it is not rude (unmannerly), and does not act unbecomingly. Love (God's love in us) does not insist on its own rights or its own way, for it is not self-seeking; it is not touchy, fretful or resentful; it takes no account of the evil done to it; pays no attention to insults and sufferings done to them from others. It does not rejoice at injustice and unrighteousness, but rejoice when right and truth prevail. Love bears up under anything and everything that comes, and is ever ready to believe the best of every person, its hopes are fadeless under all circumstances and it endures everything without weakening. Love never fails- never fades out or becomes obsolete or comes to an end. **1 Corinthians 13:4-8**

I will do what Jesus said and love my enemies, do good to those who hate me and persecute me, bless those who say bad things about me, and pray for those who mistreat me. For if I love those who love me, what is there to my credit. **Luke 6 27-28, 33**

Place me like a seal over your heart, like a seal on your arm; for love is as strong as death, its jealousy unyielding as the grave. It burns like a blazing fire, like a mighty flame. Many waters cannot quench Your love; rivers cannot quench it; rivers cannot wash it away. **Song of Songs 8:6**

The Lord has appeared to me saying: "Yes, I have loved you with an everlasting love; Therefore with loving kindness I have drawn you." **Jeremiah 31:3**

He has taken me to His banquet hall, and His banner over me is love. **Song of Songs 2:4**

I belong to my Lover and He is mine. **Song of Songs 6:3**

I will give thanks to the Lord, for He is good; His love endures forever. **1 Chronicles 16:34**

Your love, O Lord, reaches to the heavens, Your faithfulness to the skies. **Psalm 36:5**

Let love and faithfulness never leave me; I bind them around my neck, and write them on the tablet of my heart. **Proverbs 3:3**

Love and faithfulness meet together; righteousness and peace kiss each other. **Psalm 85:10**

Jesus said: "If you love me, you will obey what I command. **John 14:15**

Jesus said: "A new command I give you: Love one another. As I have loved you, so you must love one another. By this all men will know that you are My disciples, if you love one another." **John 13:34-35**

Jesus said the greatest commandment is to: "Love the Lord your God with all your heart and with all your soul and with all your mind. This is the first and greatest commandment. And the second is like it: Love your neighbor as yourself. All the Law and the Prophets hang on these two commandments." **Matthew 22:36-40**

Jesus said: "The reason my Father loves Me is that I lay down My life—only to take it up again." **John 10:17**

But God demonstrates His own love for me in this: While I was still a sinner, Christ died for me. **Romans 5:8**

The man who loves his life will lose it, while the man who hates his life in this world will keep it for eternal life. **John 12:25**

Believers overcome the devil by the blood of the Lamb, by the word of their testimony and by not loving their lives even unto death. **Revelation 12:11**

Jesus said: "As the Father has loved Me, so have I loved you. Now remain in My love. If you obey My commands, you will remain in My love, just as I have obeyed My Father's commands and remain in His love. I have told you this so that My joy may be in you and that your joy may be complete. My command is this: Love each other as I have loved you. Greater love has no one than this, that he lay down his life for his friends. **John 15:9-13**

And hope does not disappoint us, because God has poured out his love into our hearts by the Holy Spirit, whom he has given us. **Romans 5:5**

I will do everything in love. **1 Corinthians 16:14**

These three remain: Faith hope and love and the greatest of these is love. **Ephesians 5:25**

Chapter Thirteen

Humility & Meekness

Jesus said: "Whoever humbles himself like this child is the greatest in the kingdom of heaven." **Matthew 18:4**

God pours out blessings on those who are poor and realize their need for Him, for theirs is the Kingdom of Heaven. **Matthew 5:3**

God Almighty says: "This is the one I esteem; he who is humble and contrite in spirit, and trembles at My word. **Isaiah 66:2**

You hear, O Lord, the desire of the afflicted; You encourage them, and You listen to their cry. **Psalm 10:17**

Better to be lowly in spirit and among the oppressed than to share profits with those full of arrogant pride. **Proverbs 16:19**

God mocks proud mockers but gives grace to the humble. **Proverbs 3:34**

Humility and the fear of the Lord bring wealth and honor and life to me. **Proverbs 22:4**

God will give me more grace, because the Scripture says: "God opposes the proud but gives grace to the humble." **James 4:6**

Jesus said: "Unless I become humble and teachable like a little child, I shall not enter into the kingdom of heaven. Therefore, if I shall humble myself as a little child, I will become like the greatest in the kingdom of heaven. **Matthew 18:3-4**

If I exalt myself I will be humbled, and if I humble myself I will be exalted. **Matthew 23:12**

A man's pride shall bring him low: but a man of humility gains honor. **Proverbs 29:23**

I will humble myself under the mighty hand of God, that He may exalt me in due time: Casting all my care upon Him; for He cares for me. **1 Peter 5:6-7**

Blessed are the meek: for they shall inherit the earth. **Matthew 5:5**

I humble myself before the Lord, and He will lift me up. **James 4:10**

For everyone who exalts himself will be humbled, and he who humbles himself will be exalted. **Luke 14:11**

God has chosen the lowly things of this world and the despised things (and the things that are not) to nullify the things that are, so that no one may boast before Him. **1 Corinthians 1:28-29**

So neither he who plants nor he who waters is anything, but only God, who makes things grow. **1 Corinthians 3:7**

I will do nothing out of selfish ambition or vain conceit, but in humility consider others better than myself. **Philippians 2:3**

I will honor others above myself. **Romans 12:10**

I clothe myself with humility toward others, because, "God opposes the proud, but gives grace to the humble." **1 Peter 5:5**

For I do not promote myself, but Jesus Christ as Lord, for I am as a servants for the sake of Christ. **2 Corinthians 4:5**

So when I have done everything I am told to do, I will say, 'I am your unworthy servants; and have only done my duty.' **Luke 17:10**

My attitude will be the same as that of Christ Jesus; who, being in the very nature of God, did not consider equality with God something to be grasped, but made himself nothing, taking the very nature of a servant, being made in human likeness. **Philippians 2:5-7**

Humility and fear of the Lord bring wealth, honor and life. **Proverbs 22:4**

Lord, You save the humble but bring low those whose eyes are haughty. **Psalm 18:27**

Chapter Fourteen

Stewardship and Finances

By wisdom my house is built, and through understanding it is established; through knowledge the rooms are filled with rare and beautiful treasures from the Lord. **Proverbs 24:3-4**

A prudent man sees danger and takes refuge, but the simple keep going and suffer for it. **Proverbs 22:3**

Good will come to him who is generous and lends freely, who conducts his affairs with justice. **Psalm 112:5**

Lazy hands make a man poor, but diligent hands bring wealth. **Proverbs 10:4**

The sluggard craves and gets nothing, but the desires of the diligent are fully satisfied. **Proverbs 13:4**

Dishonest money dwindles away, but he who gathers money little by little makes it grow. **Proverbs 13:11**

I will waste nothing God has given me, because it is written: When they had all had enough to eat, Jesus said to His disciples, "Gather the pieces that are left over. Let nothing be wasted." **John 6:12**

I will keep my life free from the love of money and be content with what I have, because God has said, "Never will I leave you; never will I forsake you." **Hebrews 13:5**

I will take heed of warnings against foolishness and do as my Father instructs: "My son, if you have put up security for your neighbor, if you have struck hands in pledge for another, if you have been trapped by what you said, ensnared by the words of your mouth or from a pen, then do this, my son, to free yourself, since you have fallen into your neighbor's hands: Go and humble yourself; press your plea with your neighbor! Allow no sleep to your eyes, no slumber to your eyelids. Free yourself, like a gazelle from the hand of the hunter, like a bird from the snare of the fowler." Therefore, I will do everything I can to free myself of all debits and be a slave to no man. **Proverbs 6:1-5**

I am not saying this because I am in need, for I have learned to be content whatever the circumstances. I know what it is to be in need, and I know what it is to have plenty. I have learned the secret of being content in any and every situation, whether well fed or hungry, whether living in plenty or in want. **Philippians 4:11-12**

I will be rich in God and His kingdom by investing in and storing up heavenly treasures and not in the emptiness of the world which is passing away. **Luke 12:16-21**

When I want to build something, I will first sit down and estimate the cost to see if I have enough money to complete it. For if I lay the foundation and then am not able to finish it, everyone who sees it will ridicule me, saying: "This fellow began to build and was not able to finished." Therefore I will count the cost before beginning. **Luke 14:28-30**

Concerning offerings; on the first day of every week, I will set aside a sum of money in keeping with my income, saving it up, so that when missionaries & ministers come to town for offerings I can contribute so no other collections will have to be made. **1 Corinthians 16:1-2**

I will steal no longer, but work, doing something useful with my own hands, that I may have something to share with those in need. **Ephesians 4:28**

I will honor the Lord's commands and be honest with integrity. I will have accurate and honest weights and measures, so that I may live long in the land the Lord my God is giving me. **Deuteronomy 25:15**

Jesus Said: "Whoever can be trusted with very little can also be trusted with much, and whoever is dishonest with very little will also be dishonest with much. **Luke 16:10**

I will be godly with contentment which is great gain; for I brought nothing into the world, and I can take nothing out of it. If God provides food and clothing, I will be content with that. People who want to get rich often fall into temptation and led into many foolish and harmful desires that plunge themselves into ruin and destruction. For the love of money is a root of all kinds of evil. Some people are too eager for money and have wandered from the faith and pierced themselves with many griefs. Therefore I will not be like them and love money. **1Timothy 6:6-10**

I know that whoever sows sparingly will also reap sparingly, and whoever sows generously will also reap generously. Each man should give what he has decided in his heart to give, not reluctantly or under compulsion, for God loves a cheerful giver. Therefore I am going to give with great joy and freedom from conviction. **2 Corinthians 9:6-8**

Chapter Fifteen

Peace and Joy

I welcome the message of Jesus with joy by the Holy Spirit. **1 Thessalonians 1:6**

I am filled with joy because I believe. **Acts 16:34**

I am filled with joy by Your presence. **Psalm 16:11**

In the presence of the Lord is the fullness of joy. **Acts 2:28**

God has given me great joy. **Nehemiah 12:43**

I have the full measure of joy. **John 17:13**

Lord you clothe me with joy. **Psalm 30:11**

The joy of the Lord is my strength. **Nehemiah 8:10**

With joy I will be refreshed and the God of peace will be with me. **Romans 15:34-35**

With joy I will draw water, from the wells of salvation. **Isaiah 12:3**

I am awake and shout for joy. **Isaiah 26:19**

I always pray with great joy. **Philippians 1:3**

Like Jesus, I am full of joy through the Holy Spirit. **Luke 10:21**

The joy of Jesus is in me and is being made complete. **John 15:11**

No one can take away my joy. **John 16:22**

For the kingdom of God is not a matter of natural things such as eating and drinking, but is of righteousness, peace and joy in the Holy Spirit. **Romans 14:17**

You Lord turned my wailing into dancing; you removed my sackcloth and then clothed me with joy, now my heart sings to You and will not be silent. **Psalm 30:11-12**

I love righteousness and hate wickedness; therefore God sets me up above demonic forces by anointing me with the oil of gladness. **Hebrews 1:9**

I will enter Zion with singing; everlasting joy will crown my head, for gladness and joy are overtaking me, and sorrow is fleeing away. **Isaiah 35:10**

The Lord has brought me out of captivity, then He gave me great dreams and my mouth is filled with laughter, my heart consumed with songs of gladness; for the Lord has done great things for me and I am filled with overwhelming joy. **Psalm 126:1-3**

The God of hope fills me with all joy and peace as I trust in Him, so that I may overflow with hope by the power of the Holy Spirit. **Romans 15:13**

A cheerful heart is good medicine, but a crushed spirit dries up the bones. **Proverbs 17:22**

Therefore my heart is glad and my glory (my inner self) rejoices; my body too shall rest and confidently dwell in safety. **Psalm 16:9**

I am happy in my faith; I rejoice and will be happy in my heart. **1 Thessalonians 5:16**

Therefore with joy will I draw water from the wells of salvation. **Isaiah 12:3**

I delight myself in the Lord, and He will give me the desires and the secret petitions of my heart. **Psalm 37: 4**

A happy heart makes a cheerful countenance. **Proverbs 15: 13**

Because I am a believer I am happy glad, full of joy and rejoice before God. **Psalm 68:3**

This is the day the Lord has made; I will rejoice and be glad in it. **Psalm 118:24**

Heartache cruses the spirit, but a happy heart makes the face cheerful. **Proverbs 15:13**

All the days of the oppressed are wretched, but the cheerful heart has a continual feast. **Proverbs 15:15**

A cheerful look brings joy to the heart, and good news gives health to the bones. **Proverbs 15:30**

A cheerful heart is good medicine, but a crushed spirit dries up the bones. **Proverbs 17:22**

May the God of hope fill me with all joy and peace as I trust in Him, so that I may overflow with hope by the power of the Holy Spirit. **Rom 15:13**

May the God of my hope so fill me with all joy and peace in believing, through the experience of my faith, that by the power of the Holy Spirit I may abound and be overflowing and bubbling over with hope. **Romans 15:13**

The Lord makes His face shine upon me and is gracious to me; the Lord turns His face towards me and gives me peace. **Numbers 6:25-26**

For He Himself is my Peace. **Ephesians 2:14**

I turn away from evil and do good; seeking peace and pursuing it. **Psalm 34:14**

Lord, You keep me in perfect peace as my mind stays on You, because I trusts in You. This is why I put my trust in You. **Isaiah 26:3**

Jesus said: "Peace I leave with you; My peace I give to you. I do not give burdens as the world gives. So let not your hearts be troubled, neither let them be afraid. **John 14:27**

Jesus said: "I have said these things to you, that in Me you may have peace. In the world you will have tribulation. But take heart; I have overcome the world." **John 16:33**

Therefore, since I have been justified by faith, I have peace with God through our Lord Jesus Christ. **Romans 5:1**

For me to set my mind on the flesh is death, but to set the mind on the Spirit is life and peace. **Romans 8:6**

I will not be anxious about anything, but in everything by prayer and supplication with thanksgiving letting my requests be made known to

God. And the peace of God, which surpasses all understanding, will guard my heart and mind in Christ Jesus. **Philippians 4:6-7**

I rejoice in the Lord always, being full of delight by gladdening myself in Him; therefore I say to myself, rejoice! **Philippians 4:4**

Chapter Sixteen

Spiritual Warfare

The battle is the Lord's. **1 Samuel 17:47**

My enemy is the devil and his demons. **Matthew 13:37-39**

I will not be overcome by evil, but will overcome evil with good. **Romans 12:21**

For I do not fight against flesh and blood, but against principalities, against powers, against the rulers of darkness in this age, and against spiritual forces of wickedness in the heavenly realms. **Ephesians 6:12**

God has disarmed the principalities and made a bold display and public example of them, triumphing over them by the cross. **Colossians 2:15**

Therefore I will submit to God. and resist the devil by standing firm against demons, and they will flee. **James 4:7**

Jesus gave me authority to trample on serpents and scorpions, and over all the power of the enemy, and nothing shall be any means hurt me. **Luke 10:19**

Though I am human, I don't wage war with human plans and methods; instead I use God's instruments of warfare, not mere worldly weapons, to knock down demonic strongholds; breaking down every argument that keeps me from knowing God, conquering rebellious ideas and teaching my mind to obey Christ. **2 Corinthians 10:3-5**

Finally, I will be strong in the Lord and in the power of His might. I put on the whole armor of God, that I may be able to stand against the schemes of the demonic forces. For I wrestle not against flesh and blood, but against demonic forces from wicked places. Therefore I will put on the full armor of God, so that when the day of evil comes, I may be able to stand my ground, and after I have done everything to stand, I will stand firm with the belt of truth buckled around my waist, with the breastplate of righteousness in place, and with my meet fitted with the readiness that comes from the gospel of peace. **Ephesians 6:10-15**

In addition I will take up the shield of faith, which can extinguish all the flaming arrows of the evil one. Taking on the helmet of salvation and the sword of the Spirit, which is the Living Word of God. Also, I will pray in my spiritual language on all occasions to build up my spirit man, and with intense prayer I will be alert praying for others. **Ephesians 6:16-18**

I overcome demons by the blood of Jesus, by the spoken word of my testimony, and by not loving my life even to the death. **Revelation 12:11**

Jesus is the Christ, upon which I put my hope, and upon that revelation, Jesus is building His church, and the gates of hell shall not prevail against it. **Matthew 16:18**

I will be like Jesus and retreat to my secret place, my prayer closet to pray, and continue all night, fellowshipping with God the Father. **Luke 6:11-13**

This way I can watch and pray, so that I will not enter into temptation; for the spirit is willing, but the flesh is weak. **Matthew 26:41**

I will rejoice always, pray without ceasing, and in everything give thanks; for this is the will of God in Christ Jesus. **1 Thessalonians 5:16-18**

Where do fights and quarrellings come from? They come from my own evil desires, when I want something but I don't get it. When I ask and don't get what I want, it is because I ask with wrong motives, and for my own pleasures. Therefore I put off these motives and these desires I put to death that I may not fight and quarrel for my own gain. **James 4:1-3**

I will be well balanced, self-controlled and alert, because my enemy the devil prowls around like a roaring lion looking for someone to devour. Therefore, I will resist the devil, standing firm in the faith. **1Peter 5:8-9**

I am a child of God, and have overcome demonic forces, because He who is in me is greater than he that is in the world. **1 John 4:4**

Chapter Seventeen

God's Might

"At this my heart pounds and leaps from its place. Listen! Listen to the roar of His voice, to the rumbling that comes from His mouth. He unleashes His lightning beneath the whole heaven and sends it to the ends of the earth. After that comes the sound of His roar; He thunders with His majestic voice. When His voice resounds, He holds nothing back. God's voice thunders in marvelous ways; He does great things beyond our understanding." **Job 37:1-5**

No one is like You, O Lord; You are great, and Your name is mighty in power. **Jeremiah 10:6**

"Ah, Sovereign Lord, You have made the heavens and the earth by Your great power and outstretched arm. Nothing is too hard for You. You show love to thousands but bring the punishment for the fathers sins into the laps of their children after them. O great and powerful God, whose name is the Lord Almighty, great are Your purposes and mighty are Your deeds." **Jeremiah 32:17-18**

The Lord your God is with me, He is mighty to save. **Zephaniah 3:17**

"The Lord's right hand has done mighty things! The Lord's right hand is lifted high; the Lord's right hand has done mighty things!"
Psalm 118:15-16

Lift up your heads, O you gates; be lifted up, you ancient doors, that the King of Glory may come in. Who is this King of Glory? The Lord strong and mighty, the Lord mighty in battle. Lift up your heads, O you gates; lift them up, you ancient doors, that the King of glory may come in. Who is He, this King of Glory? The Lord Almighty- He is the King of Glory. **Psalm 24:7-10**

Sing to God, O kingdoms of the earth, sing praise to the Lord, to Him who rides the ancient skies above, who thunders with a mighty voice. Proclaim the power of God, whose majesty is over Israel, whose power is in the skies. You are awesome, O God, in Your sanctuary; the God of Israel gives power and strength to His people. Praise be to God! **Psalm 68:32-35**

Since my youth, O God, You have taught me, and to this day I declare Your marvelous deeds. Even when I am old and gray, do not forsake me, O God, till I declare Your power to the next generation,

Your mighty to all who are to come. Your righteousness reaches to the skies, O God, You who has done great things. **Psalm 71:18-19**

Your ways, O God, are holy. What god is so great as our God? You are the God who performs miracles; You display Your power among the peoples. With Your mighty arm you redeemed Your people. The Waters saw You, O God, the waters saw You and withered; the very depths were convulsed. The clouds poured down water, the skies resounded with thunder; Your arrows flashed back and forth. Your thunder was heard in the whirlwind, Your lightning lit up the world; the earth trembled and quaked. Your path led through the sea, Your way through the mighty waters, though Your footsteps were not seen. **Psalm 77:13-19**

Great is the Lord and most worthy of praise; His greatness no one can fathom. One generation will commend Your works to another; they will tell of Your mighty acts. They will speak of the glorious splendor of Your majesty and I will meditate on Your wonderful works. They will tell of the power and of Your awesome works, and I will proclaim Your great deeds. They will celebrate Your abundant goodness and joyfully sing of Your righteousness. I will tell of the glory of Your kingdom and speak of Your might, so that all men may know of Your mighty acts and the glorious splendor of Your kingdom. **Psalm 145:3-7, 11-12**

Your right hand, O Lord, was majestic in power. Your right hand, O Lord, shattered the enemy. In the greatness of Your majesty You threw down those who opposed You. You unleashed Your burning anger; it consumed them like stubble. By the blast of Your nostrils the waters piled up. The surging waters stood firm like a wall; the deep waters congealed in the heart of the sea. **Exodus 15:6-8**

"With my great power and an outstretched arm I made the earth and its people and the animals that are on it, and I give it to anyone I please," says the Lord. **Jeremiah 27:5**

I will fear God and give Him glory; worshipping Him who made the heavens, the earth, the sea and the springs of water. **Revelations 14:7**

Chapter Eighteen

Prophetic Revelation

May the God of our Lord Jesus Christ, the glorious Father, give me the Spirit of wisdom and revelation, so that I may know Him better; That the eyes of my heart may be enlightened in order that I may know the hope to which He has called me to partake in now, a glorious inheritance of His incomparably great power for us who believe. **Ephesians 2:17-19**

For the testimony of Jesus is the spirit of prophecy. **Revelation 19:10**

I will follow the way of love and eagerly desire spiritual gifts, especially the gift of prophecy. **1 Corinthians 14:1**

For we know in part, and we prophesy in part. **1 Corinthians 13:9**

God reveals His thoughts to me. **Amos 4:13**

God reveals mysteries to me by revelation. **Ephesians 3:3**

If a man's gift is prophesying, let him use it. **Romans 12:6**

Anyone who receives a prophet because he is a prophet will receive a prophet's reward. **Matthew 10:41**

The spirit of a prophet is subject to the control of prophets. **1 Corinthians 14:32**

Without progressive revelation the people have no restraint and perish. **Proverbs 29:18**

I receive revelation from Jesus Christ. **Galatians 1:12**

The Lord came down in the cloud and spoke with Moses, and God took of the Spirit that was on Moses and put it on the seventy elders. When the Spirit rested on them, they prophesied. **Numbers 11:25**

The Spirit of God will come upon me to prophesy just like it did King Saul when I encounter the prophets. **1 Samuel 10:10-11**

Jesus said: "Behold I stand at the door and knock. If anyone hears My voice and opens the door, I will come into him and dine with him, and he with Me."**Revelations 3:20**

After this I looked, and there before me was a door standing open in heaven. And the voice said to me: "Come up here, and I will reveal to you what must take place." At once I was in the Spirit, and before me was a throne in heaven with someone sitting on it. **Revelations 4:1-2**

Then I looked up and heard the voice of many angels, numbering thousands upon thousands, and tens of thousands times tens of thousand. They encircled the throne and the living creatures and the elders. In a loud voice they sang: "Worthy is the Lamb, who was slain, to receive power and wealth and wisdom and strength and honor and glory and praise. **Revelations 5:11-12**

Then I heard what sounded like a great multitude, like the roar of rushing waters and like loud peals of thunder, shouting: "Hallelujah! For our Lord God Almighty reigns. Let us rejoice and be glad and give Him glory! For the wedding of the Lamb has come, and His bride has made herself ready. Fine linen, bright and clean, was given for her to wear." (Fine linen stands for the righteous acts of the saints.) **Revelation 19:6-8**

Then I looked, and I saw a hand stretched out to me. In it was a scroll, which He unrolled before me. **Ezekiel 2:9**

And God said to me, "Son of man, eat what is before you, eat this scroll; then go and speak to the house of Israel." So I opened my mouth, and He gave me the scroll to eat. Then God said to me, "Son of man, eat this scroll I am giving you and fill your stomach with it." So I ate it, and it tasted as sweet as honey in my mouth. He then said to me, "Son of man, go now to the house of Israel and speak my words to them. **Ezekiel 3:1-4**

The hand of the Lord was upon me, and He brought me out by the Spirit of the Lord and set me in the middle of the valley; it was full of bones. He led me back and forth among them, and I saw a great many on the floor of the valley, bones that were very dry. He asked me, "Son of man, can these bones live? I said, "O Sovereign Lord, You alone know." Then He said to me, "Prophesy to these bones and say to them, "Dry bones, hear the word of the Lord! Be alive, and breath enters you! **Ezekiel 37:1-6**

I saw heaven standing open and there before me was a white horse, whose rider is called Faithful and True. With justice He judges and makes war. His eyes are like blazing fire, and on His head are many crowns. He has a name written on Him that no one knows but He Himself. He is dressed in a robe dibbed in blood, and His name is the Word of God. **Revelation 19:11-13**

Chapter Nineteen

Revival & Harvest

The harvest is plentiful but the workers are few. Therefore I ask the Lord of the harvest, to send out workers into his field. **Matthew 9:37-38**

Then Jesus said to me, Go! I am sending you out among the wolves. Do not take a purse or a bag or luggage, and do not be distracted by others, be focused at the task at hand. **Luke 10:2-4**

As I go, I will preach this message: The Kingdom of heaven is at hand. I will demonstrate the kingdom by healing the sick, raising the dead, cleansing those who have leprosy, and driving out demons. Freely I have received, freely I will give. **Matthew 10:7-8**

I will not procrastinate, and make excuses; I open the eyes of my heart and see the fields! Today they are ripe for harvest. **John 4:35**

I will swing my sickle, for the harvest is ripe. **Joel 3:13**

When I go into a town, I will heal the sick and tell them the kingdom of God is at hand. **Luke 10:8-9**

One sows and another reaps. He sent me to reap what I have not worked for, others have done the hard work, and I have reaped the benefits of their labor. **John 4:38**

I will take my sickle and swing, reaping a harvest, because the time has come, for the harvest of the earth is ripe. **Revelations 14:15**

I will not become weary in doing good, for at the proper time I will reap a harvest, therefore I will not give up. **Galatians 6:9**

Peacemakers who sow in peace raise a harvest of righteousness. **James 3:18**

I have received power from the Holy Spirit; therefore I will be His witnesses in Jerusalem, in Judea and Samaria, and to the ends of the earth. **Acts 1:8**

All authority in heaven and on earth has been given to Jesus. He says to me, go and make disciples of all nations, baptizing them in the name of the Father and of the Son and of the Holy Spirit, teaching them to obey everything He told us. **Matthew 28:18-20**

For God so loved the World that He gave His only begotten Son, that whoever believes in Him should not perish but have everlasting life. **John 3:16**

For all have sinned and fallen short of the glory of God. **Romans 3:23**

Jesus said, "I am the Way, the Truth, and the Life. No one comes to the Father except through Me. **John 14:6**

I will preach God's Word: "Repent therefore and be converted, that your sins may be blotted out, so that times of refreshing may come from the presence of the Lord." **Acts 3:19**

But if we walk in the Light as He is in the Light, we have fellowship with one another, and the blood of Jesus Christ His Son cleanses us from all sin. **1 John 1:7**

If we confess our sins, He is faithful and just to forgive our sins and to cleanse us from all unrighteousness. **1 John 1:9**

Chapter Twenty

The Names of God

A

ABBA .... Romans 8:15

ADVOCATE.. John 2:1

ALMIGHTY .... Genesis 17:1

ALPHA&OMEGA .... Revelation 22:13

ANCIENT OF DAYS .... Daniel 7:9

ANOINTED ONE... Psalm 2:2

APOSTLE.. Hebrews 3:1

ARM OF THE LORD................................... Isaiah 53:1

AUTHOR OF OURFAITH......................... Hebrews 12:2

B

BEGINNING & THE END .... Revelation 21:6

BRANCH... Jeremiah 33:15

BREAD OF LIFE .... John 6:35

BRIDEGROOM.. Isaiah 62:56

BRIGHT MORNING STAR .... Revelation 22:16

C

CAPTIN OF THE LORD'S ARMY........... Revelation 19:19

CHIEF CORNERSTONE........................... Isaiah 28:16

CHOSEN ONE .... Isaiah 42:1

CHRIST .... Matthew 22:42

COMFORTER.. John 14:26

COMMANDER .... Isaiah 55:4

CONSUMING FIRE.................................. Deuteronomy 4:24,
Hebrews 12:29

COUNSELOR.. Isaiah 9:6

CREATOR.. 1 Peter 4:19

D

DADDY.. Luke 23:46, Romans 8:15
DELIVERER .... Romans 11:26
DESIRED OF ALL...................................... Haggai 2:7
DOOR .... John 10:7

E

EMMANUEL .... Matthew 1:23
ETERNAL GOD... Deuteronomy 33:27
EVERLASTING FATHER .... Isaiah 9:6

F

FAITHFUL & TRUE................................... Revelation 19:11
FAITHFUL WITNESS................................ Revelation 1:5
FATHER... Matthew 6:9
FOUNDATION .... 1 Corinthians 3:11
FRIEND... Matthew 11:19

G

GENTLE WHISPER .... 1 Kings 19:12
GIVER.. Matthew 7:11
GLORY OF THE LORD .... Isaiah 40:5
GOD... Genesis 1:1
GOD ALMIGHTY...................................... Genesis 17:1
GOOD SHEPHERD .... John 10:11
GUIDE... Psalm 48:14

H

HEAD OF THE BODY .... Colossians 1:18

HEAD OF THE CHURCH........................ Ephesians 5:23

HEIR OF ALL THINGS............................ Hebrews 1:2

HIGH PRIEST .... Hebrews 3:1

HOLY ONE .... Acts 2:27

HOLY ONE OF ISRAEL .... Isaiah 49:7

HOLY SPIRIT .... John 15:26

HOPE .... Titus 2:13

I

I AM... Exodus 3:14, John 8:58

IMMANUEL... Isaiah 7:14

J

JEALOUS .... Exodus 34:14

JEHOVAH... Psalm 83:18

JESUS .... Matthew 1:21

JESUS CHRIST.. Romans 6:23

JUDGE.. Isaiah 33:22, Acts 10:42

K

KING... Zechariah 9:9

KING OF KINGS 1Timothy 6:15

KING OF THE AGES .... Revelation 15:3

L

LAMB OF GOD .... John 1:29

LAST ADAM .... 1 Cor. 15:45

LEADER.. Isaiah 55:4

LIFE .... John 14:6

LIGHT OF THE WORLD .... John 8:12

LION OF THE TRIBE OF JUDAH .... Revelation 5:5

LIVING STONE.. 1 Peter 2:4

LIVING WATER... John 4:10

LORD.. John 13:13

LORD GOD ALMIGHTY........................... Revelation 15:3

LORD JESUS CHRIST .... 1 Corinthians 15:57

LORD OF ALL.. Acts 10:36

LORD OF GLORY...................................... 1 Corinthians. 2:8

LORD OF... Haggai 1:5

LORD OF LORDS 1Timothy. 6:15

LOVE.. 1 John 4:8

M

MAN OF SORROWS................................... Isaiah 53:3

MASTER .... Luke 5:5

MEDIATOR 1Timothy 2:5

MERCIFUL GOD.. Jeremiah 3:12

MESSIAH.. John 4:25

MIGHTY GOD.. Isaiah 9:6

MIGHTY ONE .... Isaiah 60:16

MOST HIGH .... Luke 1:32

N

NAZARENE .... Matthew 2:23

O

ONLY BEGOTTEN SON .... John 1:18

P

POTTER .... Isaiah 64:8
PRINCE OF PEACE.................................... Isaiah 9:6
PURIFIER.. Malachi 3:3

R

RABBI .... John 20:16
RADIANCE OF GLORY Hebrews1:3
REDEEMER.. Job 19:25
REFINER... Malachi 3:2
RESURRECTION .... John 11:25
RIGHTEOUS ONE...................................... 1 John 2:1
ROCK 1 Cornthians10:4
ROSE OF SHARON.................................... Song of Solomon 2:1
RULER OVER KINGS OF EARTH.......... Revelation 1:5

S

SAVIOR... Luke 2:11
SERVANT .... Isaiah 42:1
SHEPHERD OF SOULS 1Peter 2:25
SHIELD .... Genesis 15:1
SON OF GOD.. Matthew 27:54

SON OF MAN .... Matthew 8:20
SON OF THE MOST HIGH........................ Luke 1:32
SOURCE.. Hebrews 5:9
SPIRIT OF GOD.. Genesis 1:2

T

TEACHER.. John 13:13
TRUE WITNESS.. Revelation 3:14
TRUTH.. John 14:6

V

VICTORY .... 2 Samuel 22:49, 1 John 5:4
VINE... John 15:5

W

WAY.. John 14:6
WONDERFUL .... Isaiah 9:6
WORD .... John 1:1
WORD OF GOD.. Revelation 19:13

Y

YAHWEH .... Exodus 6:3

Z

ZION... Psalms 2:6